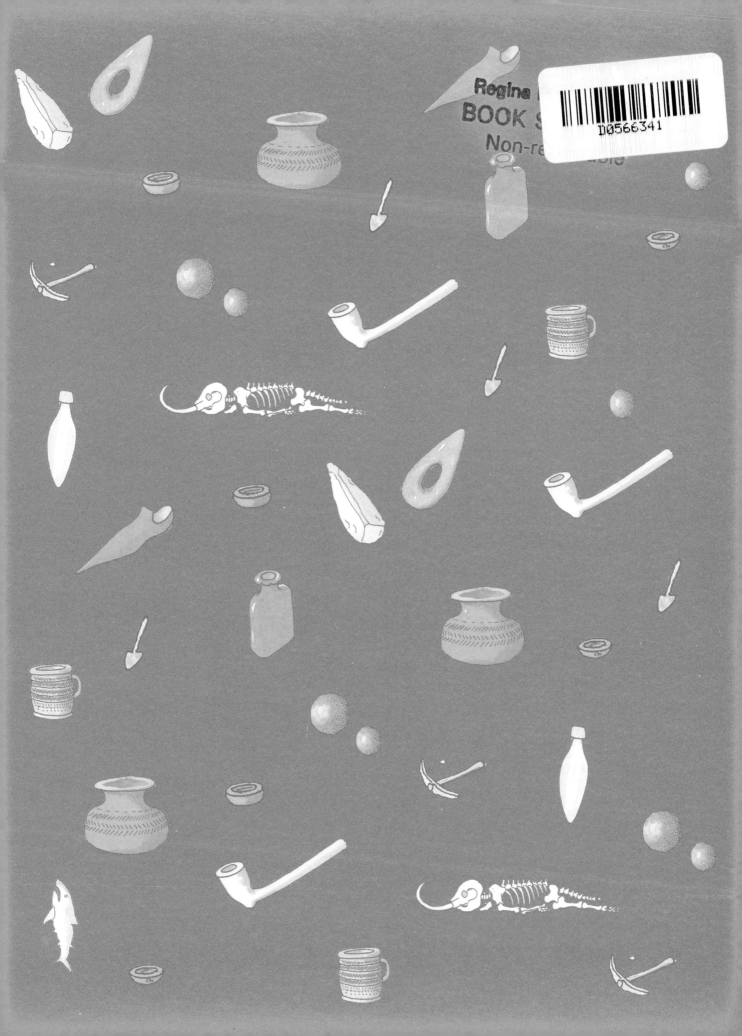

Regina
BOOK S
Non-re

CITY

ACROSS TIME

PETER KENT

CITY

ACROSS TIME →

PETER KENT

KINGFISHER
LONDON & NEW YORK

KINGFISHER
LONDON & NEW YORK

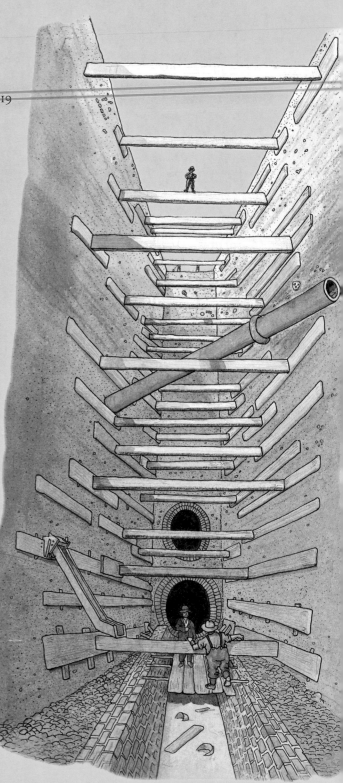

Text and illustrations copyright © 2010, 2019 by Peter Kent
Copyright © Macmillan Publishers International Ltd 2010, 2019

This edition published in 2019 by Kingfisher
120 Broadway, New York, NY 10271
Kingfisher is an imprint of Macmillan Children's Books,
London
All rights reserved.

Distributed in the U.S. and Canada by Macmillan,
120 Broadway, New York, NY 10271

Library of Congress Cataloging-in-Publication data has been
applied for.

ISBN: 978-0-7534-7520-1

Illustrations by Peter Kent
Cover Design by Laura Hall

Kingfisher books are available for special promotions and
premiums. For details contact: Special Markets Department,
Macmillan, 120 Broadway, New York, NY 10271

For more information please visit
www.kingfisherbooks.com

Printed in China
9 8 7 6 5 4 3 2 1
1TR/0619/WKT/UG/128MA

Contents

Introduction

Many towns and cities in the world are very old. In Rome, Jerusalem, Damascus, London, and other places, people have been living on the same site for thousands of years. Although most of the houses, stores, and offices you see in such ancient cities today are not much more than 100 years old, underneath them lie the remains of the buildings they replaced: layer upon layer of ruins mixed up with broken fragments of household items and garbage. Each century leaves its own layer of remains—like the age rings on a tree—the most ancient of them buried the farthest down.

The famous German archaeologist Heinrich Schliemann demonstrated this when he dug into the hill that he thought was the site of the ancient city of Troy. He was proved right, but he soon discovered that there were actually nine cities, each built on top of the remains of the one before.

This book cuts a slice through an imaginary European city where people have been living for 10,000 years. Look carefully to see how the buildings people knock down and the garbage they drop create the layers of history beneath their feet.

The first city of Troy was built around 3000 B.C., and the last was abandoned in A.D. 500. Can you imagine how many layers there would be if Troy were still lived in today?

The 19th century
The 18th century
The 17th century
The 16th century
The Middle Ages
The Dark Ages
The Romans
The Iron Age
Stone Age

IX 150 B.C. – A.D. 400

VIII 900–150 B.C.

VII 1250–1000 B.C.

TROY VI 1800–1250 B.C.

V 2100–1800 B.C.

IV 2300–2100 B.C.

III 2500–2300 B.C.

II 2500 B.C.

TROY I 2920–2500 B.C.

Schliemann and the treasures of Troy

6

Treasure trove

Archaeologists love rubbish—the more ancient, the better. The objects they find in the layers beneath the city give valuable clues about dates and important events. A layer of ash tells us that there was once a great fire in the city; skeletons with the markings of sword cuts and arrowheads show war and massacre. But the real importance of the things archaeologists find is that they help us understand how people in the past lived their everyday lives.

When a Stone Age woman threw out a broken pot, she did not realize that her refuse would be carefully examined and glued back together thousands of years later. Even something very small, like a button, can tell us a lot about the people who made it. It gives us an idea of what type of clothes they wore, how skilled they were at making things, and, if it is not made of a material found locally, it tells us how far the people traveled and traded.

Thousands of objects are buried beneath the city in this book, just waiting to be discovered. If you look carefully through the slices of the city depicted, you will find all the things on this page.

It was fashionable in the Middle Ages to wear very long, pointed shoes. Some shoes were so long that they had to be tied to the leg with a chain. Shoes at this time were not made for left and right feet, and most had no heels.

Tobacco was first brought to Europe from America in the 16th century (1500s). It was smoked in pipes made of baked clay. People thought it was good for their health.

In the 17th century (1600s), cannons fired solid iron balls. The largest weighed 64 lb. (29kg) and were 8 in. (200mm) wide, but 18 lb. (8 kg) balls were more usual. They are still dug up from old battlefields.

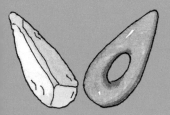

Stone axes from the Stone Age were not always rough or crude. Many were polished and ground to a jewel-like finish.

Pots have always been used for storing food and for eating and drinking from. Stone Age pots were made out of clay and decorated with patterns. They were then baked hard in a kiln.

In the Iron Age, people displayed their wealth as jewelry. A rich person would wear magnificent gold necklaces and armlets called torques.

The Romans were skilled at making stone and bronze statues. Some were huge, designed to stand on monuments or in temples, but many were small ornaments for the home.

Doctors and pharmacists in the 18th century (1700s) made their own medicines. A blue bottle often meant that the contents were poisonous.

Digging down through history

The people who dig to look for the remains of our history are called archaeologists. They love it when an old building is knocked down because then they get the chance to look at what lies beneath its foundations. They measure and sketch plans of any ruins and carefully excavate the soil to find as many objects as they can, all of which are then carefully photographed and labeled. The archaeologists usually have to work quickly because the owners of the site are impatient to start work on their new building, and when they do, any ruins will be buried or destroyed.

A theodolite is used to survey the site and figure out heights and levels.

A temporary office is used to store records and carry out scientific tests.

The sides of the excavation are drawn to scale and photographed.

Pottery is washed and sorted.

A ground radar cart measures the depth of buried objects.

It is very important to record exactly where everything is found and what it looks like in order to figure out how old it is.

Labels mark features such as floors and layers.

A measuring pole is used to show scale in photographs.

Small objects are carefully uncovered with trowels and brushes.

A sieve is used to collect very small objects.

9

The old Stone Age

The period of time more than 3,000 years ago is called the Stone Age because the tools that people used then were made of stone. At the beginning of the Stone Age, people traveled around the countryside with their possessions in search of food. About 10,000 years ago, the last ice age ended and the huge sheets of ice that had covered most of Europe and America retreated back to the north. The warmer climate encouraged small groups of people to travel northward from the south.

Many of the animals that roamed the land at this time—woolly mammoths, giant elk, woolly rhinoceros, and aurochs (large wild cows)—are now extinct. There were no cities. People moved across the land in search of food, living off wild plants and the animals they killed. They had no houses and lived in simple shelters made from branches or animal hides that could easily be taken down when it was time to move on. You can still find arrowheads and axes where the people left them, and that is all that remains . . . except for their paintings.

Cave paintings

The people of the Stone Age did not usually live in caves—they were too dark and damp—but they did use them as secret temples and holy places. On the walls they painted beautiful pictures of animals and hunting scenes. These may have been part of a magic ceremony to make sure that there would always be plenty of animals to hunt so that they would never go hungry. They used colors made from soil, mixed with animal fat, and they drew outlines with charcoal sticks or soot.

The new Stone Age

During the last part of the Stone Age, people learned how to grow crops and keep animals. This meant that they could live in one place. They built simple houses out of wood, mud, and thatch (straw or other plant material).

Stone Age people's knives, axes, spearheads, and scrapers were made from stone—usually flint—and they had also learned how to tame dogs to help them hunt. When they could not find enough flint on the ground, they dug pits to mine it. Needles and small tools were made out of animal bone. Deer antlers were used as picks, and oxen's shoulder blades were used as shovels. As stone and bone tools were lost or thrown away, they became buried underground. It is the remains of these objects that archaeologists look for today.

Cooking the Stone Age way

Just imagine how difficult it must be to cook without any metal pots or an oven. This is how it was done around 2000 B.C.

1. Wrap a joint of meat in straw.

2. Fill a huge trough with water and put the meat in it.

3. Boil the water by dropping in red-hot stones.

4. After about 3½ hours, the meat is ready.

12

Stone circles

The greatest monuments of the Stone Age in Europe are the stone circles. We do not know their real purpose, but they were probably used as giant calendars to mark the seasons and religious festivals. At a stone circle in Avebury, England, a skeleton was found under one of the fallen stones. It was the remains of a 17th-century farmer. He was trying to break up the stone when it toppled over and crushed him.

13

The Iron Age

Around 2000 B.C., people discovered how to make tools out of metal. At first they used copper, but it was very soft. Then they learned how to mix tin with copper to make bronze, which was harder. Around 800 B.C., people began to make tools and weapons out of iron, which was the strongest metal of all.

Iron Age towns were often protected by strong walls made of timber and earth. Houses were larger and more comfortable than they were during the Stone Age. By now, people had learned how to weave cloth and make beautiful jewelry out of gold and silver. They sold their goods outside their town and also bought goods from distant places. Money was used for the first time instead of simply swapping goods. Iron bars were used as money at first, but they were later replaced by gold coins.

Blue tattoos
The people of the Iron Age painted or tattooed themselves with intricate swirling patterns drawn in a blue vegetable dye called woad.

War chariots
Chariots were used in Iron Age warfare.
Warriors ran down along the harness pole
of the chariot as it was being driven at full
speed, ready to fight their enemies.

Ancient Roman times

By about A.D. 100, the mighty Romans had conquered most of Europe and made it part of their vast empire. The Romans constructed the first buildings made of brick and stone in what is now Great Britain and France.

A Roman town had a central market and meeting place called a forum, as well as a town hall, many stores, paved streets, and public baths with hot water and central heating. The bigger towns had several temples and an amphitheater where games and fights between gladiators took place. The Romans knew that clean people were healthier, so they built sewers and organized a good supply of fresh water in towns.

Smelly pots
Although the Romans were eager to keep clean, their apartment buildings (below left) must have been very smelly. There were no toilets, and urine was collected in big pots at the bottom of the stairs. The urine was sold to clothmakers to stiffen fabric.

Keeping out burglars

The Romans did not have a real police force and were worried about being burgled. They built their houses with only a few windows on the walls facing the street, and they put complicated locks on their doors. In many houses, the door was jammed shut with a pole.

Household gods

Every Roman home had a shrine and an altar dedicated to the household gods. The head of the family made an offering there every day to keep in favor with them.

Waiting for water

Only the richest people had water piped directly into their houses. Most people got their water from public fountains. These must have been very social places where people gossiped as they waited in line.

The catacombs

The Romans did not allow dead people to be buried inside the city, so all the cemeteries were outside the city walls. Bodies were cremated, or burned, on a pyre and the ashes placed in a special jar called an urn.

A secretive sect who worshiped the god Mithras met in underground temples (left). The chief worshiper dressed up as lions and ravens to make offerings to Mithras, who was always shown killing a bull.

Christians were not popular at first in Rome. Many were persecuted (ill-treated) because they would not worship pagan gods. They were forced to hold services in secret, hidden away deep in the catacombs (below).

The urns were then placed inside or underneath beautiful monuments that were often decorated with a statue or bust of the dead person.

When space ran out above ground, cemeteries called catacombs were built underground. Long passages were excavated, and the funeral urns were placed in niches in the walls, similar to books on a shelf. Richer people had large chambers where the entire family could be buried.

The ashes in a funeral urn were placed in a prepared niche during a solemn ceremony.

The Dark Ages

During the A.D. 400s, the Roman Empire, which had been growing weaker for a century, was invaded by tribes from northern Europe known as barbarians. The barbarian tribes that settled within the old empire—the Goths, Franks, and Saxons—did not want to live in the Roman towns, and the buildings quickly fell into ruin.

The barbarians could not build with stone at first, and their houses were usually made of wood with thatched roofs. The hall of the chief, or "thegn," was the most important building in any village. The leader lived in this hall with his warriors.

Stone crosses
The barbarians were pagans, worshiping many gods, until they were converted to Christianity. One of the first things the Christians did was to erect a stone cross, normally on the site of a pagan holy place. This is where a church was later built.

Saxon treasure
The Saxons were skilled jewelry makers. Wealthy men and women wore beautiful brooches, clasps, and pendants. They were often made of gold and decorated with glass or colored stones.

Learning to build
When the Franks and the Saxons began to build in stone around A.D. 700, they copied the Roman ruins around them. Their early attempts were much less sophisticated than the Romans'.

The Middle Ages

During the Middle Ages (roughly A.D. 1000 to 1500), towns grew and became rich again. Throughout much of Europe, houses were made of wooden frames with plaster walls. Only castles, churches, and the houses of the very wealthy were built of stone. The streets were often unpaved, with open drains, and it was difficult to keep the town clean. Animals wandered around, and people threw garbage out their windows.

The marketplace was very important. People came in from the countryside to sell food and buy goods made in the town. Stores were simple rooms that opened out onto the street. Almost all of the things sold in a store were made in the house behind.

Soccer

A favorite street game was soccer. Sometimes hundreds of people played in one game! It was noisy and dangerous—houses were damaged and people killed.

Miracle plays

People were very religious during the Middle Ages, and they celebrated holy days with feasts and festivals. Miracle plays were popular, and groups of townspeople would work together to put on a particular scene.

A medieval mine

Mining has always been a dirty and dangerous job, ever since the new Stone Age, when men dug deep into chalk for the biggest and best flints. Ancient Egyptians mined gold, and the Romans dug for copper, gold, iron, and lead all over their empire. In the Middle Ages, the most skilled miners were to be found in Germany, where they invented many amazing machines to make their work easier.

This horse-powered pump uses three pistons to raise the water.

Water continually seeped into the mine and had to be pumped out. This pump is made of an endless chain of wooden buckets powered by a hand crank and simple gears.

A winch lifted the silver ore up the main shaft from the mine.

Spaces where ore had been dug out were filled with waste rock.

The miners wore a linen coverall with a hood. You can see how this inspired the costume of the dwarfes in the Walt Disney movie *Snow White and the Seven Dwarfs*.

Poisonous gases were always a danger, so small birds were used as gas detectors. If the bird fell unconscious, the miners knew that dangerous gas was present.

This picture shows a silver mine. Miners had to dig deep to reach the precious ore—the rocks that contained the silver. Coal mining did not become important until most of Europe's forests had been cut down and burned as fuel.

A water-powered fan pushed fresh air down the shaft to enable the miners to breathe.

The silver was present in the ore, which had to be brought to the surface and crushed.

The first railroads were used in German mines. The rails and wheels of the trucks were made of wood.

A fire was lit to get air moving through the tunnels.

The miners climbed up and down the shaft on ladders. Sometimes they slid down poles or even down a leather carpet.

Before drills and explosives were invented, miners split large rocks using wooden wedges.

Props made of wood held up the roof. Often they bent or broke under the weight of the rocks above.

The mine was lit by simple oil lamps.

The 16th century

By the sixteen century (1500s), houses were larger and had chimneys instead of just a hole in the roof. Most windows were filled with glass for the first time rather than being closed with wooden shutters. Although still built mainly from wood, houses were more comfortable and contained more furniture and ornaments.

The city's streets were still unpaved, dirty, and littered with garbage. At night, the city was dark and often dangerous. Fresh water was taken to houses by a person who worked as a water carrier or was fetched by the family from a fountain (unless a house had a well). There were no real drains, and during the summer, the city was very smelly and unhealthy.

Public punishment
Criminals were often whipped
through the streets or
put in the stocks
(right) to have
rotten vegetables
thrown at them.

The 17th century

Very few European cities survived the 17th century (1600s) without being entirely or partially destroyed by fire. Often the cause was accidental, but many cities were burned down after being bombarded or captured by enemies. Soldiers who captured cities also badly damaged them as they searched every house for things to steal.

Outbreaks of the plague killed thousands of people. The plague was mainly spread by rats, which made their nests in the wooden houses and fed on the garbage that lay in the streets.

Firefighting
Long hooks pulled burning thatch off roofs. Fire engines were simple hand pumps.

Plague pits

So many people died from the plague that they were buried together in huge pits.

The 18th century

The great fires of the 17th century meant that many cities were almost completely rebuilt during the 18th century (1700s). Most of the old wooden buildings were replaced by houses built of brick and stone. This new style of architecture was based on copies of Roman buildings. Roads were now paved, and parts of the city began to be less cramped as wide streets and broad squares were built.

Sedan chairs
Wealthy people rode in a sedan chair through crowded city streets. They could be hailed like taxis can today.

Watchmen

There was still no police force in cities, so the streets were patrolled by watchmen. A popular sport for young men was to knock over the watchman's shelter and roll him down the street in it!

The 19th century

During the 19th century (1800s), cities changed more than at any other time in their history. They grew much larger, and all types of different buildings were constructed. There were train stations, concert halls, libraries, offices, and schools. The streets were better paved and brightly lit by gas lamps. Underground pipes carried gas and water into the city and sewage out of it. Cities became healthier and less smelly places to live in, but they suffered from a new problem--traffic jams!

Drain

Pneumatic postal railroad

32

Water
pipe

Gas pipe

Sewer

33

An underground railway

One hundred and fifty years ago the streets of London, England, were crammed with horse-drawn carts, carriages, and buses. They moved at a slow crawl, and the noise and smell was overpowering. Something needed to be done or the streets would be jammed solid. A network of undergound roads in tunnels lit by gaslight was suggested, but the police objected: thieves and muggers would lurk in the shadows.

A better solution was an underground railway, or subway, beneath the overcrowded streets to carry workers smoothly into the city. It took almost 20 years to plan and build the Metropolitan, the world's first underground railway. It was 4 mi. (6km) long and was an instant success when it opened in 1863.

The railway was only 33 ft. (10m) underground and built by the "cut and cover" method. A deep trench was dug, the rails were laid, and then a brick arch was built to complete the tunnel. The trains were pulled by steam locomotives that were supposed to be smokeless, but they still filled the tunnels with choking fumes. At stations there were openings to the streets above to let in light and air.

Small railroad cars powered by compressed air carried mail bags in a tube beneath the streets at 6 mph (10km/h).

EXIT

First Class

Steam locomotives could not be used on routes deep underground. These lines had to wait until new methods of tunneling and electric trains were invented (right). The first deep line or "tube" opened in London in 1890. The passenger cars had no windows—as there was nothing to look at—and were pulled by little electric locomotives. Later lines had trains of cars with electric motors—like the ones in use today.

The 20th century

Duthe 20th century (1900s), wars and new construction destroyed many old buildings. Some of those that remained were altered to suit new uses. Below the streets, more tunnels carried extra drains as well as electricity, telephone, and television cables.

36

Some cities developed public subway systems in tunnels deep underground. Many buildings rose to great heights, with deep foundations to support their weight. The workers who dug these foundations sometimes helped archaeologists by finding ancient remains in the oldest parts of the cities.

Secret bunker

For more than 40 years, starting in 1945, the U.S. and other Western powers confronted the U.S.S.R. in what was known as the Cold War.

Both sides threatened each other with atomic bombs powerful enough to destroy entire cities. Huge bunkers were built deep underground, where people would be safe from blasts and deadly radiation. It was much too expensive to build shelters like this for everyone, but it was important to make sure that the government and military command would survive so that there would not be complete chaos after the bombs had dropped.

Entrance one

Subway

Dormitory

Cafeteria

Kitchen

Recreation room

This bunker in a secret location was made of two parallel tubes 130 ft. (40m) below the ground. There was room for about 500 people, plus all the communication equipment they would need in order to stay in contact with other bunkers and keep the country running. They had supplies for up to six months, as it would have been too dangerous to come to the surface any sooner.

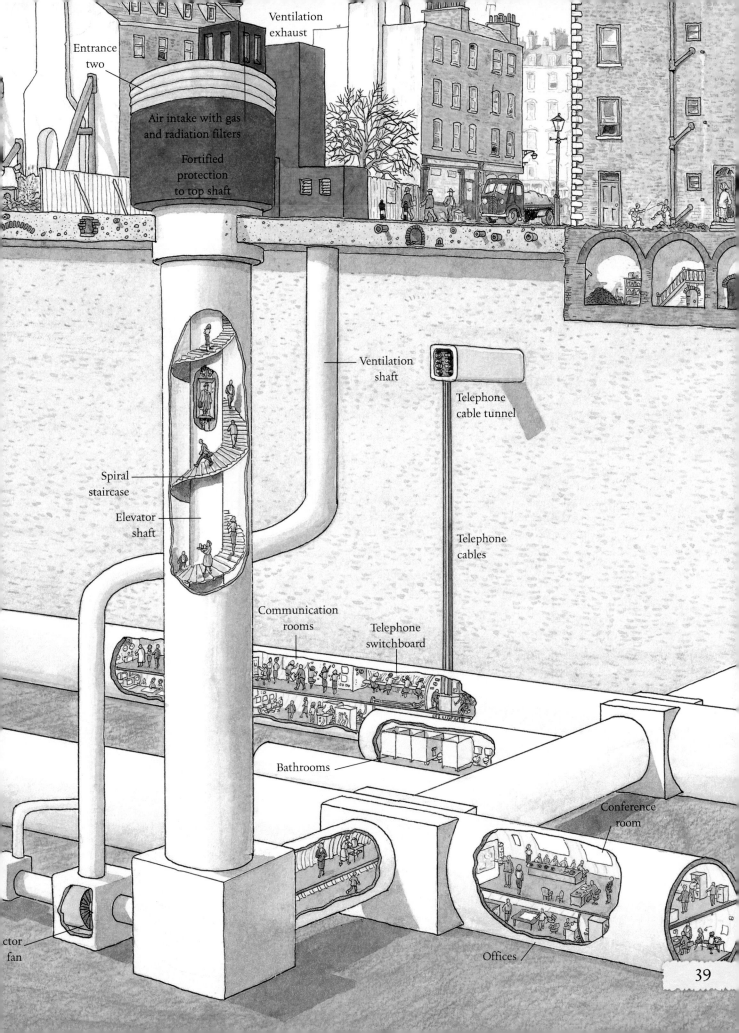

Entrance two

Ventilation exhaust

Air intake with gas and radiation filters

Fortified protection to top shaft

Ventilation shaft

Telephone cable tunnel

Telephone cables

Spiral staircase

Elevator shaft

Communication rooms

Telephone switchboard

Bathrooms

Conference room

...ctor fan

Offices

39

The 21st century

Cities will be greener 50 years from now. Nonpolluting electric transportation will make the air clean and clear again. New buildings will be designed to use very little energy and to make the most of wind and solar power, while beautiful old buildings will be cherished and put to new uses.

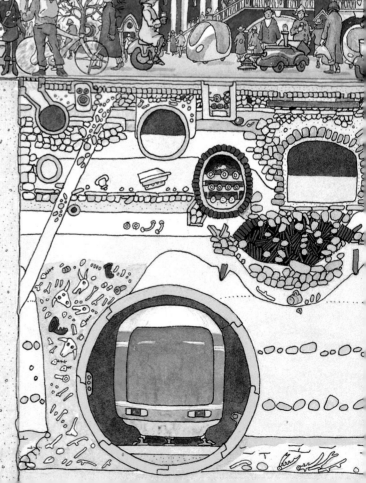

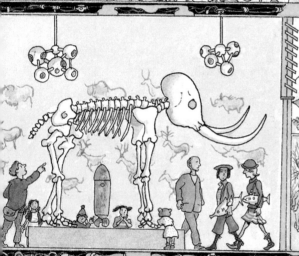

he purpose of the city will
emain much the same: it
ill be a place to live,
ork, shop, and be
ntertained—
ust as it
as been
hroughout
s history.

The distant future

Who knows what our city will look like in 10,000 years? Perhaps war or climate change will have destroyed it so completely that nothing remains on the surface except the stumps of mighty buildings, weathered and overgrown to look like hills.

But if, even further in the future, civilization starts again or aliens arrive to explore the planet, the archaeologists of the distant future will find plenty to keep them busy as they cut a slice through what used to be a city.

43

Glossary

Archaeology The study of the past by digging up objects and the remains of buildings.

Archaeology

Barbarians The tribes who lived outside the borders of the Roman Empire and who appeared rough and uncivilized to the Romans.

Bunker An underground shelter made of reinforced concrete or some other material strong enough to resist bombs and shells.

Catacomb An underground cemetery. A catacomb has long tunnels with tombs and chambers for burials dug into the sides. Catacombs are very useful for burying large numbers of people without taking up too much room above ground.

Crank Part of an axle bent at a right angle. It is useful for changing back-and-forth or up-and-down movement into a circular motion—like the pedals on a bike.

Crank

Foundations The lowest part of a building that gives firm support to the walls.

Locomotive An engine that moves under its own power. The term usually refers to the engine that pulls a train along a railroad track. Locomotives are powered by electricity, diesel, steam, and—occasionally—compressed air.

Locomotive

Mithras A Sun god from ancient Persia. He is usually shown as a young man wearing a pointed cap and killing a bull. His worshipers met in underground temples and dressed up as lions and ravens for their secret ceremonies. Nobody worships Mithras today.

Mithras

Niche A shallow recess in a wall designed to hold a statue, vase, or ornament.

Ore A rock that contains particle of some useful material, such as iron, copper, or gold. Usually it has to be crushed or melted to separate the metal from the surrounding rock.

Ore

Pagan Someone who doesn't believe in Christianity or one of the other major religions. The pagans of the past worshiped many gods and goddesses, including Jupiter, Mercury, Thor, and Freya.

Pagan

Pendant An ornament usually attached to a necklace, chain, or cord and hanging down over the chest.

Pharmacist A person who mixes up and sells medicinal drugs. Before the 19th century, such professionals were often called apothecaries. They were less scientific than pharmacists are today.

Pharmacist

ague A rapidly spreading infectious disease. Usually refers to bubonic or pneumonic plague: the Black eath of the Middle Ages that killed about one-third all the people in Europe and kept recurring until e 1800s.

yre A pile of wood on hich to burn a dead body.

Pyre

adar A device to detect objects sending out radio waves. When e waves hit something solid, they ounce back, and the machine can ad the signals to determine the size, shape, d position of the object. Radar is mostly used airplanes and ships, but archaeologists find dar very useful to detect things underground.

ewage Technically anything carried in a sewer underground channel, but it usually means uman waste.

haft A vertical or sloping entrance to a mine. he vertical shafts of gold mines in South frica are up to 9,840 ft. (3,000m) deep.

Shaft

Shrine A place for religious objects and holy statues where people pray and make offerings to a god or gods.

Solar power Electricity made from the heat and light of the Sun.

Switchboard In an old-fashioned telephone system, every phone had a wire that led to a board, where it ended in a socket. If you

wanted to speak to someone at another phone, the switchboard operator plugged a wire into your socket and then plugged it into the socket of the number you asked for, and the connection was made.

Switchboard

Theodolite An instrument with a rotating telescope used by surveyors to measure horizontal and vertical angles. It is essential for setting out the levels for new roads and buildings.

Treasure trove A discovery of buried valuables. Specifically, the term refers to a discovery of gold or silver that has been hidden for a very long time by an unknown owner who is not likely to claim it. Things that have just been lost are not treasure trove. Different governments have their own laws about what treasure trove is and whether the finder is allowed to keep the valuables.

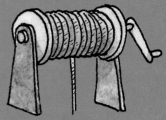
Treasure trove

Urn A vase, usually with a rounded base, used for storing the ashes of a dead body.

Winch A machine for lifting in which the rope or wire is wound around a roller or drum. Another name for this is a windlass.

Winch

Shrine

Index

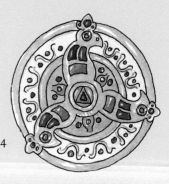

Further information

You can go online to find a wealth of information on European archaeological finds and see photos of real artifacts. If you are interested in history and archaeology in general, visit digs and events in your local area.

The old Stone Age
France has some of the most beautiful and impressive cave paintings in the world, and most are in southwestern France. The most famous site is the cave at Lascaux. For a virtual tour, go to **archeologie.culture.fr/lascaux/en**

The new Stone Age
See photos and read about a real Stone Age flint mine at **www.megalithic.co.uk/article.php?sid=4800** Explore the famous monument Stonehenge at **www.english-heritage.org.uk/visit/places/stonehenge/ history-and-stories/stonehenge360**, and read about other stone circles at **www.stonepages.com**

The Iron Age
At Castell Henllys near Newport, Wales, an Iron Age fort has been rebuilt with ramparts, round houses, and a granary to show what it was like in 500 B.C. See it online at **https://www.pembrokeshirecoast.wales/default.asp?PID=261**

Ancient Roman times
There are Roman remains all over Europe. After London, England, was bombed during World War II, a lot of the Roman city was revealed beneath the rubble of modern buildings, including a complete temple of Mithras. See images and videos and learn about the process of digging up Roman remains at **www.museumoflondon.org.uk/discover/ paternoster-square-roman-london**

The catacombs
The best catacombs are in Rome, Italy. You can read about them at **www.catacombe.roma.it/en/le-origini-delle-catacombe.php** and **www.nationalgeographic.com/history/ancient/ catacombs.html**

The Anglo-Saxons
Sutton Hoo, a famous archaeological site in England, tells us a great deal about the Anglo-Saxons of the Dark Ages. See pictures of armor, jewelry, and other artifacts at **www.earlybritishkingdoms.com/kids/sutton_hoo.html**. The huge Anglo-Saxon treasure trove unearthed in 2009 in Staffordshire, England, will help archaeologists learn even more. Read about this exciting discovery and see photos at **www.staffordshirehoard.org.uk**

Medieval mines
One of the best preserved medieval mines in the world is the World Heritage site of Banská Stiavnica, in Slovakia. Kraków, Poland, has amazing salt mines, with more than 600 mi. (1,000km) of tunnels up to 1,000 ft. (300m) below ground. For a good list of historic mines in Europe, including photos and links, see **https://www.erih.net/i-want-to-go-there/list/Sites/// mining**

Medieval to modern times
Many museums in Europe feature good displays of archaeological artifacts from all periods. If you plan to visit, check out the directory at **www.inexhibit.com/specials/museums-archaeology-archaeological-sites-around-world** Archaeological museums in the United States and Canada often focus on North America's own fascinating history. To find events and exhibits in your area, go to **www.saa.org/education-outreach/public-outreach/ centers-public-archaeology**

An underground railway
The first underground railway is now part of the Circle Line on the London Underground in England. For more information on the history of the Underground, go to **https://tfl.gov.uk/ corporate/about-tfl/culture-and-heritage/londons-transport-a-history/london-underground/a-brief-history-of-the-underground**

Secret bunker
During the Cold War with the U.S.S.R., the U.S. government kept a top-secret underground bunker in the mountains of West Virginia. Learn more about it at **www.atomicheritage.org/history/greenbrier-bunker**

The 21st century
To get an idea of how buildings might look 30 years from now, go to **www.bbc.co.uk/news/technology-23524249**

Digging down through history
There are archaeological digs going on all the time, and some even welcome volunteers to help. For more information on North American digs and discoveries, plus interactive digs throughout history, go to the Archaeology Institute of America's website: **www.archaeology.org**. For a database of world archaeological sites, see **www.archiuk.com/archi/archi_search_world.html**

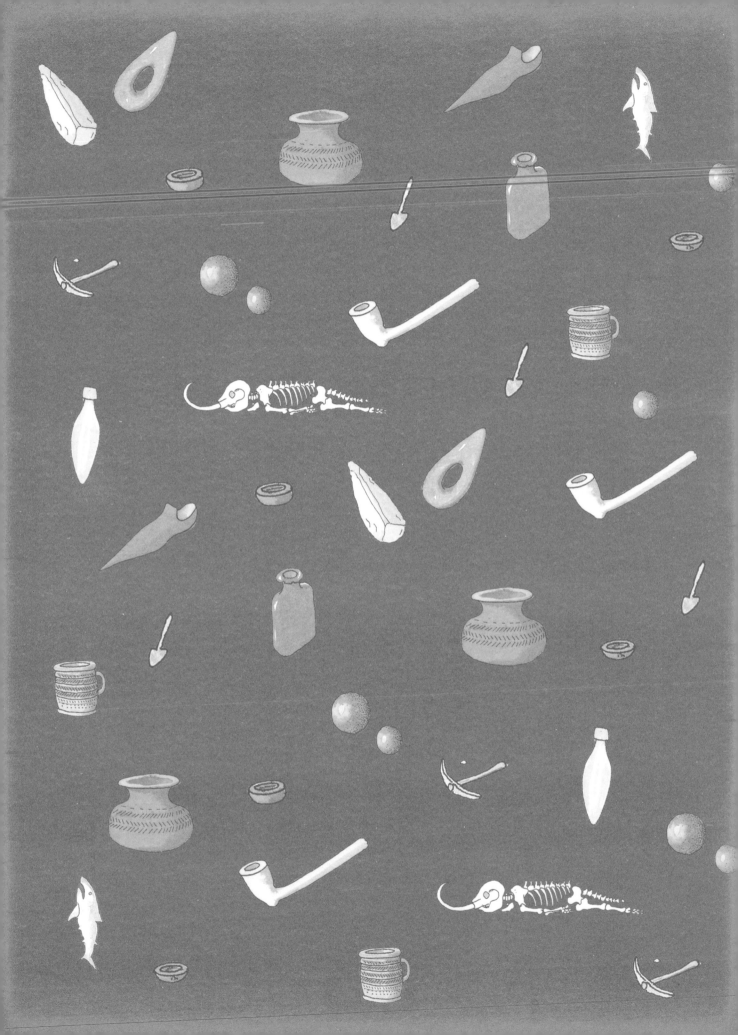